❦ Metric Munchies for Junior Cooks ❦

MORE KIDS IN THE KITCHEN

Shannon Ferrier and Tamara Shuttleworth

Foreword by Elizabeth Baird

James Lorimer & Company, Publishers
Toronto 1980

Contents

Foreword 3
Introduction 5
1. Biscuits and Breads 7
2. Light Dishes 13
3. Salads and Vegetables 22
4. Main Dishes 35
5. Sweets and Treats 49
Go-Togethers 60
Measures 62
Baking Pan Sizes 62
Temperature Conversion 62
Index 63

Copyright © 1980 by Shannon Ferrier and Tamara Shuttleworth. All rights reserved. No part of this book may be reproduced or transmitted in any form or by any means, electronic or mechanical, including photocopying, or by any information storage or retrieval system, without permission in writing from the publisher.

ISBN 0-88862-386-0 cloth
      0-88862-385-2 spiralbound

Cover design: Hans Zander

Design: Don Fernley

Text illustrations: Sheila Shapira.

6 5 4 3   83 84 85 86

Canadian Cataloguing in Publication Data

Ferrier, Shannon.
   More Kids in the Kitchen

(Kids of Canada)

ISBN 0-88862-386-0 bd.   ISBN 0-88862-385-2 pa.

1. Cookery-Juvenile literature. I. Shuttleworth, Tamara. II. Title. III. Series.

TX652.5.F468   j641.5'123   C80-094568-9

James Lorimer & Company, Publishers
Egerton Ryerson Memorial Building
35 Britain Street
Toronto M5A 1R7, Ontario

Printed and bound in Canada

Foreword

For the kids who loved *Kids in the Kitchen* here is a second volume of great Canadian cooking and eating. Thousands of youngsters have already learned their basics and enjoyed the tremendous pleasure of cooking thanks to Shannon Ferrier's first book, *Kids in the Kitchen*. Now she has teamed up with her sister to produce this larger collection of delectable and healthy recipes.

All of the recipes are very clear and easy to follow. Each one has a complete list of ingredients and tools plus detailed and to-the-point cooking instructions. There are symbols — "E" for easy, "M" for medium and "H" for hard — to help junior cooks and adults make a wise choice of recipes. The format of *More Kids in the Kitchen* will also encourage young cooks to develop good kitchen organizational skills. For safety's sake, Mom or Dad should decide just how closely they want to supervise operations, but parents won't have to worry about interpreting recipes. These recipes are written especially for kids to understand. No doubt parents *will* want to help eat the finished products!

The selection of recipes in *More Kids in the Kitchen* opens up wonderful possibilities, not only for cooking adventures but also for broadening children's understanding of our cultural heritage. There is a nice selection of time-tested Canadian specialties, such as those summertime favourites, Corn on the Cob; Tea Biscuits; Devilled Eggs for picnics; East Coast Chowder; slow-cooked French-Canadian Baked Beans and Grandma's Bran Muffins, dark and rich with lots of bran, molasses, walnuts and raisins.

Then there's a marvelous range of recipes that reflect our thriving multicultural make-up. Among these are spicy Jamaican Patties, perfect for parties; creamy Noodles Alfredo; Greek Tomato Salad with black olives and feta cheese; Chinese Chicken Wings; a luscious Cheesecake Pie; Quick Beef Curry and Chapatis. And as if this weren't enough, the authors present a selection of healthy versions of ever-popular junk foods — Super Burgers, Fresh Fruit Milkshakes and Allison's Chocolate Chip Cookies.

On the theme of nutrition, *More Kids in the Kitchen* categorizes each recipe into its food group or groups according to *Canada's Food Guide*. However, this cookbook is refreshingly free from the heavy-handed approach to nutrition often associated with encouraging children to eat well. The emphasis here is not on a rigid pattern of "musts" but on delicious recipes for good food. There are lots of recipes for salads and vegetables, especially fresh ones; and where appropriate, recipes use wheat germ and whole wheat flour. Milk, cheese and yogurt make frequent appearances in the recipes, and there are plenty of good main course recipes featuring meat and fish. Dessert recipes are made with wholesome ingredients, and they deliver much more than empty calories. The authors have created a series of sample menus to help fledgling cooks balance meals nutritionally, using new and interesting dishes. It won't take long for children to discover that this book is full of good things to eat and that good ingredients mean good food.

Lastly, *More Kids in the Kitchen*, like *Kids in the Kitchen*, takes a practical and fun approach to cooking that comes from the authors' years of experience in teaching children how to cook. Shannon and Tamara know from their own children, friends and a multitude of happy students not only what kids like to eat, but what kids like to cook. They know how to present recipes that children understand and, what's more, enjoy making.

Elizabeth Baird

Introduction

This is a book about good things to cook. Each recipe tells you what foods and tools you'll need and exactly what to do with them. Most of the recipes are easy enough to make yourself, but be ready for everyone to want to help when it's time to eat.

If you are just learning how to cook, start with a recipe marked "E" for easy. When you feel ready, go on to the recipes marked "M" for medium and then "H" for hard. After you've had some practice cooking single recipes, you can try making a whole meal. The recipes are also marked with symbols to show the food groups they represent.

MILK and MILK PRODUCTS

FRUITS and VEGETABLES

MEAT and ALTERNATES

BREAD and CEREALS

For a well-balanced meal choose foods from different groups. Remember, for good health you need a variety of foods from each group every day.

On page 60 you'll find a list of Go-Togethers. These are suggestions for dishes that taste especially good when served at the same meal. Many of the recipes have been brought to Canada from other countries. Have fun trying them in the menus we recommend. You'll discover many more delicious combinations of your own.

Last but not least — a word about safety. Kitchen tools can be dangerous. Use knives and electrical appliances with care and always be sure to use oven mitts or potholders when handling anything hot. For beginning cooks it's a good idea to have an adult nearby in case you need help.

Happy cooking, happy eating.

Shannon Ferrier
Tamara Shuttleworth

For our children — Allison, Tamara and Peter Elijah

 Biscuits and Breads

Grandma's Bran Muffins

These muffins will give you a taste of pioneer life. Canada's early settlers used hearty ingredients to make chewy muffins chock-full of energy. If they aren't all eaten hot out of the oven, store the rest in a covered container for breakfast.

Food

- 15 mL butter
- 500 mL bran
- 250 mL all-purpose flour
- 10 mL baking soda
- 250 mL raisins
- 125 mL chopped walnuts
- 75 mL vegetable oil
- 100 mL molasses
- 375 mL plain yogurt

Tools

- muffin pan (for 12 muffins)
- measures
- large bowl
- wooden spoon
- rubber scraper

Here's How

1. Set the oven at 200°C.
2. Use the 15 mL butter to grease the muffin pan.
3. Measure the bran, flour, baking soda, raisins and walnuts into the bowl. Stir.
4. Make a hole in the flour mixture and pour the vegetable oil, molasses and yogurt into it. Mix together just until the dry ingredients are moistened. Do not overmix.
5. Spoon the batter into the muffin pan and bake for 20 minutes.
6. Remove the muffins from the pan to cool.

Tea Biscuits

What's in a name? In England these biscuits are called oven scones, but since they tasted so good with a cup of afternoon tea, Canadian settlers soon dubbed them "tea" biscuits. In the United States, where tea is a less popular drink, they're called baking powder biscuits.

Food

500 mL all-purpose flour
 20 mL baking powder
  2 mL salt
100 mL shortening
200 mL milk
 10 mL all-purpose flour

Tools

measures
large bowl
fork
pastry blender or 2 knives
wooden board
round biscuit cutter
(about 5 cm in diameter)
baking sheet

Here's How

1. Set the oven at 220° C.
2. Mix the 500 mL flour, baking powder and salt in the bowl.
3. Put the shortening into the bowl and use the pastry blender to cut it into the flour until the mixture is crumbly. (If you don't have a pastry blender you can do this with 2 knives.)
4. Add the milk and stir lightly with a fork until just blended.
5. Sprinkle the board with 10 mL flour. Turn the dough out onto the board and knead it about 8 times by pulling it toward you with your fingertips, then gently pushing it down and away.
6. Pat down the dough until it is about 1.5 cm high. Cut it into rounds with the biscuit cutter and place them on the ungreased baking sheet. Gather up the scraps of dough and gently pat them out again so all the dough can be cut into rounds. You'll have about 18 biscuits. Bake for 12 to 15 minutes and serve warm with butter.

HINT: Once you've discovered how easy this basic recipe is, you'll want to try some of these tempting variations:

1. **Cheese Biscuits**
   Add 250 mL grated cheddar cheese to the flour mixture in Step 2.

2. **Bacon Biscuits**
   Add 125 mL crumbled cooked bacon just before you add the milk in Step 4.

3. **Whole Wheat Biscuits**
   Replace the 500 mL flour with 250 mL all-purpose flour and 250 mL whole wheat flour.

4. **Speedy Drop Biscuits**
   Instead of kneading and patting the dough, drop it by spoonfuls onto the ungreased baking sheet.

5. **Campfire Biscuits**
   Instead of kneading and patting the dough, shape spoonfuls of it around the end of a long stick of green wood and cook over a campfire until light brown and crusty.

HOW TO CUT IN SHORTENING WITH A PASTRY BLENDER AND 2 KNIVES.

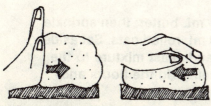

HOW TO KNEAD THE DOUGH

Oatmeal Batter Bread

Who says all loaves of bread have to look alike? This one, baked in a bowl, will be wonderfully round. Canada first learned to like oats when Scots settlers brought their recipes for oatmeal porridge, oatcakes and oatmeal breads.

Food

250 mL rolled oats
300 mL milk
 50 mL butter
 50 mL warm water
  5 mL white sugar
 15 mL dry yeast
       (1 package)
 15 mL butter
 50 mL rolled oats
 75 mL molasses
  1   egg
  7 mL salt
375 mL all-purpose flour
300 mL whole wheat flour

Tools

measures
large bowl
small pot
mixing spoon
glass measure
2 L casserole or oven-proof bowl
plate
wire rack

Here's How

1. Put the 250 mL rolled oats into the large bowl.
2. Measure the milk and butter into the small pot and place it over high heat. When the mixture starts to boil, carefully pour it over the rolled oats. Let it cool.
3. Stir the sugar into the warm water in a glass measure. Stir in the yeast and let stand 10 minutes until the mixture is bubbly. Stir again to make sure the yeast is dissolved.
4. Grease the casserole with 15 mL butter; then sprinkle the sides and bottom with 50 mL rolled oats. Set aside.
5. Add the molasses, egg, salt and yeast mixture to the oats in the large bowl. Stir well. Add the flours and mix thoroughly.

6. Spoon the batter into the casserole dish. Cover it with a plate turned upside down. Set it on a counter away from drafts for 45 minutes or until the batter has doubled in size. (It should rise to the top of the casserole.)
7. Preheat the oven to 180°C. Remove the plate; then bake the bread for 45 to 50 minutes. The loaf should sound hollow when it is tapped lightly. Cool the bread in the casserole for 10 minutes; then remove it to a wire rack to finish cooling.

Chapatis

A favourite bread in India, these crisp whole wheat pancakes are perfect with spicy curry. They taste best freshly cooked, so prepare them just before you sit down to your Indian dinner.

Food
500 mL whole wheat flour
3 mL salt
175 mL water
25 mL whole wheat flour
butter

Tools
measures
medium bowl
mixing spoon
wooden board
clean tea towel
rolling pin
heavy frying pan
lifter
knife

Here's How

1. Mix the 500 mL flour and salt in the bowl. Stir in the water, a little at a time, to make a firm dough.
2. Sprinkle the 25 mL flour on the board. Knead the dough on the board for about 3 minutes until you can form a smooth ball. (See illustration, p.9.) Cover it with the towel and let it sit for 30 minutes.
3. Divide the dough into 10 pieces. Roll each into a ball; then use the rolling pin to roll each ball into a thin round on the floured board. If the dough sticks, sprinkle more flour on the board. Each chapati will be about 14 cm across.
4. Put the frying pan over medium-high heat. Place one chapati in the ungreased pan. Cook it for 1 minute until lightly browned; then turn it over to brown the other side for 1 minute. Turn the chapati once more and leave it for a few seconds while it puffs up slightly. Remove it from the pan and spread lightly with butter. Cook the other chapatis the same way and serve at once.

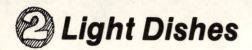# Light Dishes

Hard-Cooked Eggs

What could be easier than hard-cooked eggs? And once you've learned the trick, you'll be able to make delicious Egg Salad (p. 14) or Devilled Eggs (p. 15). Or use them to garnish French Potato Salad (p. 29).

Food
eggs (as many
as you need)
water

Tools
large pot with lid
slotted spoon
large bowl

Here's How

1. Fill the pot half full of cold water.
2. Carefully place the eggs in the water, making sure they are completely covered.
3. Slowly bring the water to a boil. Put the lid on the pot and turn off the heat. Let the pot sit for 20 minutes.
4. Use the slotted spoon to lift the eggs into the bowl. Fill the bowl with cold water to cool the eggs.
5. Drain the water from the bowl and refrigerate the eggs until you're ready to use them.

Egg Salad

This is a salad you can eat in a sandwich. Moist and creamy, it's a super filling for toasted whole wheat bread or a bagel. Forget the bread and scoop egg salad onto a lettuce leaf with sliced tomatoes, cucumber and cheese, and you'll have a nice light lunch. This recipe makes enough for 2 sandwiches or 2 salads or 1 of each.

Food

- 3 hard-cooked eggs (p. 13)
- 25 mL mayonnaise
- 1 green onion
  or
- 15 mL finely chopped celery, chives, sweet pickles or cooked ham

Tools

- small bowl
- fork
- cutting board
- knife
- measures

Here's How

1. Peel the hard-cooked eggs and mash them well in the bowl with a fork.
2. Wash the green onion and chop it finely. Stir the mayonnaise and onion (or one of the alternate ingredients) into the eggs. Refrigerate the egg salad mixture if it isn't served immediately.

Devilled Eggs

What's so devilish about these eggs? Perhaps it's the spices mashed into the yolk or the bright red paprika you can sprinkle on top. However they got their name, these eggs make a tasty picnic treat. But keep them chilled until you're ready to eat because mayonnaise spoils easily on a hot summer day.

Food
- 6 hard-cooked eggs (p. 13)
- 50 mL mayonnaise
- 2 mL salt
- 1 mL pepper
- 1 mL mustard
- paprika

Tools
- knife
- small bowl
- fork
- measures
- small spoon
- plate

Here's How
1. Peel the eggs. Cut them in half lengthwise.
2. Remove the yolks, being careful not to break the whites.
3. Mash the yolks in the small bowl with the mayonnaise, salt, pepper and mustard.
4. Use the small spoon to scoop the yolk mixture back into the egg whites. Sprinkle the yolks *very* lightly with paprika.
5. Place on a serving plate.

HINT: Use fresh parsley or lettuce under the eggs to make your dish look more attractive.

Cooked Rice

Cooking rice is like a magic trick. When you finally lift the lid — presto! — there's three times as much rice as when you started. But that's okay. You can always use the extra to make Fried Rice (p. 17). There's no need to wash rice before cooking. If you do, you'll rinse valuable nutrients down the drain.

Food

250 mL white rice (not the fast-cooking kind)
500 mL cold water
 15 mL butter
  5 mL salt

Tools

measures
heavy pot with lid
fork

Here's How

1. Measure the rice, water, butter and salt into the pot.
2. Put on the lid and place the pot on a burner at high heat. As soon as the water begins to boil, turn the heat down as low as possible.
3. Let the rice cook for 20 minutes without lifting the lid.
4. Use a fork to fluff up the rice before serving. This amount of rice will make 4 servings, or about 750 mL cooked rice.

HINT: If you want to use brown rice, you will need to cook it for 15 to 25 minutes longer. Brown rice includes more of the outer layers (and more of the nutrients) of the natural rice. These layers take longer to cook. Brown rice is not recommended for the Fried Rice recipe in this book.

Fried Rice

More than half the families in the world eat rice every day. In the Orient rice grows in paddies, flooded fields where farmers work ankle-deep in water. But rice can also be grown on dry land like many other grains. This recipe shows you how to make a popular Chinese dish. Small amounts of meat, eggs and vegetables add colour, flavour and food value to the rice.

Food

   3   strips bacon
750 mL cooked rice (p. 16)
   3   eggs
   3   green onions
 15 mL vegetable oil
125 mL frozen peas
 15 mL soya sauce

Tools

cutting board
knife
frying pan
wooden spoon
2 small bowls
fork
measures

Here's How

1. Chop the bacon into small pieces. Place it in a large frying pan and stir over medium heat until cooked but not crisp. Leave the bacon fat in the pan but remove the bacon to a small bowl.
2. Break the eggs into another small bowl and scramble them with a fork. Wash and slice the green onions; add them to the eggs.
3. Cook and stir the egg-onion mixture in the frying pan until the eggs set. Break it into small pieces with the fork and add it to the bowl containing the bacon.
4. Place the vegetable oil, the cooked rice and the frozen peas in the frying pan. Cook over medium heat, stirring until the peas are heated through, about 5 minutes.
5. Add the cooked bacon, eggs and onion to the frying pan. Stir in the soya sauce. When well mixed, serve at once. Serves 6.

Favourite Pancakes

Almost every country makes its own version of this ancient delicacy. In Christian countries families traditionally made pancakes on Shrove Tuesday to use up extra eggs and fat before the fasting of Lent began. Today pancakes are a favourite treat in every season.

Food

375 mL all-purpose flour
 25 mL white sugar
 15 mL baking powder
  3 mL salt
375 mL milk
 50 mL vegetable oil
  1   egg
  5 mL vegetable oil

Tools

measures
large bowl
mixing spoon
medium bowl
frying pan
paper towel
lifter
cookie sheet

Here's How

1. Measure the flour, sugar, baking powder and salt into the large bowl. Stir.
2. Mix the milk, 50 mL oil and egg in the medium bowl.
3. Add the milk mixture to the flour mixture and stir lightly, just enough to blend the ingredients. The batter should be a little bit lumpy.
4. Use the 5 mL oil to grease the frying pan; then wipe it lightly with a paper towel.
5. Set the frying pan over medium-high heat. (Set an electric frying pan at 190°C.) The pan is ready when a drop of water will sizzle on it.
6. Use a 50 mL measure to drop the batter into the pan. When the pancakes start to bubble in the centre and dry on the edges, turn them over carefully to cook the other side. Turn only once.
7. Keep the cooked pancakes warm on a cookie sheet in a 100°C oven while you finish cooking the rest. Serve them hot with butter and syrup. This recipe makes about 12 pancakes.

HINT: Pancakes are delicious plain, but for a change try:
Blueberry Pancakes
Just add 250 mL fresh or frozen blueberries to the batter before cooking.

Maple-Flavoured Syrup

In the early spring, when the days are sunny and the nights are cold, the sap begins to rise in the sugar maple trees. Canada's native people discovered that this clear, watery sap could be boiled to make a rich, dark syrup. But it takes more than 30 litres of sap to make 1 litre of syrup, and today real maple syrup is too expensive for everyday use. Try to visit a sugar bush next spring to see how the sap is gathered and to taste the fresh, light sweetness of the new syrup. In the meantime surprise your family with this delicious substitute.

Food
125 mL corn syrup
125 mL brown sugar
125 mL water
 10 mL butter
  5 mL maple flavouring

Tools
measures
medium pot
wooden spoon

Here's How

1. Measure the corn syrup, sugar and water into the pot. Bring it to a boil over high heat, stirring constantly. Remove it from the heat at once and stir in the butter and maple flavouring.

HINT: This makes a great sundae poured on ice cream and topped with chopped nuts.

Jamaican Patties

Meat pies are made all over the world. In Jamaica meat pies called "patties" are sold in bake shops for lunches or snacks. If you like spicy food, you may want to add a chopped fresh chili pepper the way most Jamaicans do. But try the milder recipe first.

Food

For the Filling
- 1 large onion
- 15 mL vegetable oil
- 500 g ground beef
- 5 mL salt
- 5 mL curry powder
- 3 mL thyme
- 2 mL pepper
- 100 mL bread crumbs
- 250 mL water

For the Pastry
- 500 mL all-purpose flour
- 10 mL baking powder
- 5 mL curry powder
- 2 mL salt
- 2 mL turmeric
- 150 mL shortening
- 50 mL butter
- 125 mL cold water

Tools

knife
cutting board
frying pan
measures
lifter

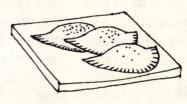

measures
large bowl
pastry blender (or 2 knives)
fork
wooden board
rolling pin
knife
baking sheet

Here's How

1. Peel the onion; then chop it into small pieces. Place it in the frying pan with the oil and ground beef and cook over medium heat until the meat is browned, about 5 to 10 minutes. Use the lifter to stir the meat.
2. Add the salt, curry powder, thyme and pepper. Cook and stir for 1 minute. Add the bread crumbs and stir; then add the water. Cook over low heat for another 2 or 3 minutes. The mixture should not be watery. Set aside.
3. Measure the flour, baking powder, curry powder, salt and turmeric into the large bowl.
4. Add the shortening and butter, cutting them into the flour mixture with the pastry blender or 2 knives until it resembles course crumbs. (See illustration, p. 9.)
5. Add the cold water, stirring with the fork until you have a ball of dough. Divide it into 16 equal portions and set aside.
6. Set the oven at 180°C. You'll need a small glass of water and about 50 mL flour to assemble the patties.
7. Sprinkle a little flour (about 15 mL) on the wooden board and rolling pin. Take one small portion of dough and flatten it between your hands; then roll it out to a thin circle about 16 cm in diameter.
8. Place a scoop (about 40 to 50 mL) of the meat mixture on the circle. Then dip your finger into the glass of water and use it to moisten the edges of the dough. Fold the circle in half, covering the meat, and press the edges together with a fork.
9. You now have a half-moon shape that can be trimmed cleanly with a knife if the edges are a little ragged. Prick through the top crust with a fork and place the patty on the baking sheet. Continue making the rest of the patties in the same manner, sprinkling more flour on the board if the dough begins to stick.
10. Bake for 25 to 30 minutes until the crust is cooked and lightly browned. Serve hot or cold.

Salads and Vegetables

Cucumber–Yogurt Salad

This cool salad is a refreshing treat with a serving of spicy food like curry. Children in Russia, Greece and India enjoy slightly different versions of this international favourite.

Food
   1   large cucumber
250 mL plain yogurt
   2 mL lemon juice
   1 mL dill weed
        a sprinkle of salt
        and pepper

Tools
vegetable peeler
cutting board
knife
small spoon
measures
mixing bowl

Here's How

1. Peel the cucumber and cut it in half lengthwise. Cut each half in half again and carefully scoop out the seeds with the spoon.
2. Chop the cucumber into tiny pieces and place in the mixing bowl.
3. Add the yogurt, lemon juice, dill weed, salt and pepper to the bowl. Stir well; then refrigerate until ready to use.
4. To serve, pour into a pretty glass bowl. This recipe makes 4 healthy servings.

Greek Tomato Salad

Not all salads are made of lettuce. This one, popular in Greece, is not a green salad at all. The vivid red, black and white of tomatoes, olives and feta cheese will make a colourful change for your table.

Food
- 5 ripe tomatoes
- 250 mL feta cheese
- 12 small black olives
- 25 mL olive oil
- 25 mL wine vinegar
- 5 mL dried basil
- 2 mL salt
- 1 mL pepper

Tools
- cutting board
- knife
- large plate
- measures

Here's How
1. Wash the tomatoes. Slice them into rounds and arrange them on a large plate.
2. Crumble the cheese over the tomatoes and decorate with the black olives.
3. Sprinkle the oil, vinegar, basil, salt and pepper evenly over the salad. Serve at once. Makes 4 servings.

Great Garden Salad

Lettuce comes from a large family. Make your salads with romaine, endive, escarole, iceberg or Boston lettuce. Or combine more than one kind. They like to get together.

Food

1 head of lettuce
8 radishes
2 green onions
1 stalk of celery
1 small cucumber
2 tomatoes
1 recipe of Red French Dressing (p. 28)

Tools

paper towels
salad bowl
cutting board
knife
vegetable peeler
2 forks

Here's How

1. Remove any damaged outer leaves of lettuce. Wash the lettuce under cold running water. Drain well and pat dry with paper towels. (For leafy lettuce such as romaine, separate the leaves and wash each one thoroughly; then pat dry.) Tear the lettuce into bite-size pieces and place in the salad bowl.
2. Wash the radishes, green onions, celery, cucumber and tomatoes.
3. Slice the radishes thinly. Chop the green onions and celery into small pieces. Peel the cucumber and slice it into thin rounds. Cut the tomatoes into 8 wedges each.
4. Add all of the cut-up vegetables to the salad bowl. Toss lightly with 2 forks to mix. Add the salad dressing and toss lightly again. Serve at once. This makes about 6 servings.

HINT: Any combination of fresh vegetables can be used. Try grated carrot, chopped green pepper, small cauliflower pieces or sliced raw mushrooms.

Fresh Vegetables for Dips

A colourful plate of crisp vegetables and a cool, tasty dip make a tempting snack. Make your arrangement interesting by using different colours and a variety of shapes, such as strips, rounds or chunks.

Food
Any combination of celery, carrots, radishes, turnip, green peppers, cauliflower, cucumber, cherry tomatoes, raw mushrooms

Tools
cutting board
knife
vegetable peeler
bowl
measures
large plate

Here's How

1. Thoroughly wash all of the vegetables except the mushrooms; then prepare each as follows:
   Celery — Trim the ends of the stalks. Cut each stalk into finger-length sections; then cut each section into 2 or more lengthwise strips. Or cut the stalks crosswise into 3 cm chunks.
   Carrots — Peel. Cut in half crosswise, then again lengthwise. With the cut surface down, cut each piece into narrow lengthwise strips. Or cut each carrot into thin diagonal slices to form ovals.
   Cucumber — Peel only if the skin has been waxed. Slice crosswise into thin rounds.

HOW TO CUT VEGETABLES

Green Peppers — Cut in half and remove the seeds; then cut into lengthwise strips.
Turnip — Cut a 1 cm slice from the turnip. Peel it; then cut it into strips about 1 cm wide.
Cauliflower — Remove all leaves; then break the cauliflower into small "flowers".
Cherry Tomatoes — Leave them whole.
Radishes — Cut off the stems and root tips.
Mushrooms — Wipe them clean with a damp paper towel and serve whole.
2. Keep each type of vegetable refrigerated in a separate plastic bag until you're ready to arrange them on a large plate.

HINT: Don't stop here. How about trying raw green beans, broccoli, green onions, asparagus, zucchini or Chinese pea pods?

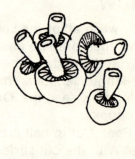

Three-Cheese Dip

If you like cheese, you'll love this thick dip, which uses three of the most popular cheeses made in Canada. Try it with raw vegetables, crackers or chips.

Food

125 mL	cheddar cheese (finely grated)
½	small onion (about 15 mL chopped)
1	small carton of cottage cheese (250 g)
1	small package of cream cheese (125 g)
15 mL	mayonnaise
5 mL	Worcestershire sauce

Tools

grater
cutting board
knife
measures
large bowl
electric mixer
serving bowl

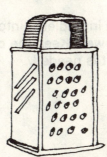

Here's How

1. Grate the cheddar cheese. Peel the onion and then chop it finely.
2. Measure all of the ingredients into the bowl and beat with the mixer until they are well blended.
3. Refrigerate the dip for at least 30 minutes before using to bring out the flavour.
4. Spoon the dip into an attractive bowl for serving. This makes about 500 mL of dip.

Red French Dressing

How do you dress a salad? Not in jeans and running shoes. Try this delicious French dressing that really puts the "Great" in Great Garden Salad (p. 24).

Food

  50 mL vegetable oil
  25 mL vinegar
  15 mL ketchup
   2 mL salt
   1 mL pepper
   1 mL white sugar

Tools

  measures
  small jar with lid

Here's How

1. Measure all of the ingredients into the jar. Close the lid tightly and shake well. Keep the dressing in the refrigerator until it is needed.

June's Coleslaw

In Magnetawan, Ontario, June makes bowls and bowls of coleslaw to serve in her restaurant. The kids think it's the best cabbage salad they've ever tasted. Now June is sharing her recipe with kids all over Canada. The recipe makes at least 12 servings, so invite some friends to help you eat it. Or store the left-over coleslaw in a covered container in the refrigerator. It will keep fresh for a month.

Food
- 125 mL white sugar
- 125 mL white vinegar
- 3 mL mustard seed
- 3 mL celery seed
- ½ medium cabbage
- 2 medium carrots
- 1 medium onion
- 2 stalks celery (about 250 mL chopped)
- ½ green pepper

Tools
- measures
- small pot
- vegetable peeler
- grater
- large bowl
- cutting board
- knife
- spoon

Here's How

1. In the small pot boil together the sugar, vinegar, mustard seed and celery seed for 5 minutes. Let it cool.
2. Remove any wilted outer leaves from the cabbage. Wash the cabbage, carrots, celery and green pepper. Peel the carrots and onion.
3. Grate the cabbage, carrots and onion into the large bowl.
4. Finely chop the celery and pepper and add them to all the ingredients together well.
5. Pour the vinegar mixture over the vegetables and mix all the ingredients together well.
6. If you're not serving this salad immediately, keep it refrigerated in a covered glass or plastic container.

French Potato Salad

In France potato salad isn't made with mayonnaise dressing. Children there expect a *vinaigrette*, a mixture of oil and vinegar. Try the French version to see which you like best. Mix the ingredients while the potatoes are still warm so that the potatoes can absorb more of the interesting flavours. New potatoes keep their shape best for this dish.

Food
- 6 medium potatoes
- 5 mL salt
- water
- 2 green onions
- 75 mL olive oil
- 40 mL wine vinegar
- 2 mL salt
- 1 mL pepper
- 2 hard-cooked eggs (p. 13)
- 15 mL chopped parsley

Tools
- measures
- large pot with lid
- cutting board
- knife
- small bowl
- spoon
- colander
- serving bowl

Here's How

1. Wash the potatoes and put them into the large pot with 5 mL salt. Cover them with water; then put a lid on the pot and bring the water to a boil. Cook for 15 minutes or until just tender. Be sure not to let them get too soft.
2. Meanwhile, wash and finely chop the green onions. Mix them in the small bowl with the oil, vinegar, salt and pepper. Set aside.
3. Drain the potatoes in the colander; then rinse them with cold water until they're not too hot to handle. Peel them, cut into slices and place in the serving bowl.
4. Pour the oil mixture over the potatoes. Stir very gently to mix.
5. Peel and slice the eggs. Arrange them over the potatoes. Sprinkle with the chopped parsley. Serve warm immediately or chill for later use. Serves 6.

Corn on the Cob

In the long Canadian winter we dream of summer food: ripe, red tomatoes, fresh blueberries, strawberries and, of course, hot buttered corn on the cob. Long before Europeans arrived in the Americas, the native people knew the glories of corn. They cooked it in the husk over campfires or ground it between stones to make cornmeal. Cook it indoors or out, but don't let summer slip by without lots of corn on the cob. You'll have to dream again next winter.

Food
water
fresh ears of corn (1 or 2 per person)
soft butter
salt
pepper

Tools:
For Boiling
large pot with lid
tongs

For Barbecuing
squares of aluminum foil
pastry brush
tongs

Here's How:

To Boil Corn
1. Fill the pot half full of water and bring the water to a boil.
2. Remove the husks and silk from the corn. Using the tongs, carefully put the ears of corn into the water.
3. Cover the pot and bring the water to a boil again. Cook the corn for 5 to 8 minutes until tender.
4. Lift out the corn and serve at once with lots of butter, salt and pepper.

To Barbecue Corn
1. Remove the husks and silk from the corn and place each ear on a square of foil.
2. Brush the ears of corn with butter and sprinkle with a little salt. Roll the foil tightly around the corn and twist the ends to seal.
3. Cook on the barbecue grill for 10 to 15 minutes, turning each ear often.
4. Serve hot with more butter, salt and pepper.

Baked Potatoes with Onion

Potatoes, like corn, were grown by the native people of South America long before Europeans knew that potatoes or corn existed. Now the nutritious potato is cooked in different ways all over the world. This recipe with onions is delicious with any kind of meat. The potatoes can be cooked on a barbecue if you wrap them in two layers of foil.

Food

    4   large potatoes
    2   onions
    50 mL butter (melted)
         sour cream

Tools

cutting board
knife
measures
small pot
aluminum foil

Here's How

1. Set the oven at 200°C.
2. Wash the potatoes well. Make deep cuts in each potato about 1 cm apart but not all the way through.
3. Peel the onions; then cut them into thin slices. Put a slice of onion into each cut in the potatoes.
4. Melt the butter over low heat in the small pot.
5. Place each potato on a large square of aluminum foil. Carefully pour the melted butter over the potatoes so that it drips into the cuts. Fold the foil around each potato and pinch the ends together at the top to seal.
6. Bake the potatoes for 45 minutes. Serve them hot with sour cream.

HINT: If you are already baking something in the oven at 180°C, you can put the potatoes in at the same time and bake them for 1 hour.

HOW TO CUT POTATOES

Stir-Fried Broccoli

A fast cooking method used by the Chinese for centuries, stir frying guarantees healthy vegetables because they are never overcooked. Teach your family to eat this dish with chopsticks.

Food

500 g	broccoli (about 4 or 5 stalks)
1	clove garlic
30 mL	vegetable oil
1	chicken bouillon cube (the soft kind, which is easy to crumble)
15 mL	water

Tools

knife
cutting board
measures
frying pan with lid
lifter

Here's How

1. Wash the broccoli. Cut the stems in diagonal slices about 1 cm thick. Cut the top into separate "flowers". Set aside.
2. Peel the garlic clove and chop it into very tiny pieces.
3. Pour the vegetable oil into the frying pan; then place the pan over high heat. Add the garlic and use the lifter to stir it quickly until it begins to turn golden (about 1 minute).
4. Add the broccoli and stir quickly for 2 minutes.
5. Crumble the bouillon cube over the broccoli, turn the heat down to medium and stir for another 2 minutes.
6. Add the water and cover the frying pan with a tight-fitting lid. Turn the heat to medium-low and let the broccoli steam for 1 minute. Serve at once. Makes 4 servings.

HINT: This recipe also works well with fresh green beans.

Sweet and Sour Red Cabbage Ⓜ

We like to eat what looks good, and red cabbage adds a nice touch of colour to this popular German dish. It's a perfect partner for roasts or sausages. The "sweet" and the "sour" make a tangy blend for the taste buds.

Food

- 50 mL butter
- 1 onion
- 1 medium red cabbage
- 2 apples
- 50 mL brown sugar
- 50 mL vinegar
- 50 mL raisins
- 50 mL water
- 5 mL salt
- 1 mL pepper

Tools

- measures
- large pot with lid
- wooden spoon
- cutting board
- knife

HOW TO REMOVE CABBAGE CORE.

Here's How

1. Melt the butter in the pot over medium heat.
2. Peel and chop the onion; then cook it with the butter for 5 minutes, stirring occasionally.
3. Remove the outer leaves of the cabbage; then cut it into quarters and remove the core. Slice the cabbage pieces finely and add to the pot.
4. Wash the apples. Then cut them into quarters and remove the cores. Chop the apples and add to the pot.
5. Add all of the other ingredients to the pot and stir well.
6. Cover the pot and cook over medium heat for 30 minutes. Stir once during the cooking. Makes 6 servings.

Main Dishes

Chinese Chicken Wings

Good hot or cold, these wings may be eaten as a main course or a snack. Serve them with Fried Rice (p. 17) and Stir-Fried Broccoli (p. 33) to treat your family to a Chinese meal.

Food
- 10 chicken wings
- 50 mL white sugar
- 50 mL soya sauce
- 5 mL vegetable oil
- 5 mL garlic powder

Tools
- knife
- cutting board
- large bowl
- measures
- baking pan

Here's How

1. Cut the wings at the joints so that each is in 3 sections. Discard the wing tips.
2. Place the wing pieces in the large bowl with the sugar and soya sauce. Stir to make sure the meat is well coated.
3. Let this mixture sit in the refrigerator for at least 30 minutes, stirring occasionally to keep the wings coated with sauce.
4. Preheat the oven to 180°C. Grease the baking pan with the vegetable oil.
5. Arrange the wings in a single layer in the pan, pouring any extra liquid on top. Sprinkle the garlic powder over the wings and bake for 45 minutes, turning once after 20 minutes. If the pan juices begin to dry up, add a little water and stir. Serves 4 or 5.

Noodles Alfredo

Alfredo and his noodles were a famous pair in the cooking circles of Rome, Italy. And so this recipe was soon called Noodles Alfredo. But before you make it, you'll have to learn to say *fettucine*. That's the type of Italian egg noodles you'll be using. Noodles Alfredo has a Canadian cousin, macaroni and cheese, but wait till you taste the difference. With a salad this dish makes a perfect light meal, or serve it as a separate course during a big dinner.

Food

	water
10 mL	salt
15 mL	vegetable oil
1	package of fettucine or broad egg noodles (about 500 g)
125 mL	butter
125 mL	heavy cream (35%)
125 mL	grated Parmesan cheese
50 mL	grated Parmesan cheese
25 mL	finely chopped parsley

Tools

large platter
large pot with lid
measures
wooden spoon
small pot
colander
2 forks

Here's How

1. Set the platter in a 100° C oven to keep warm.
2. Fill the large pot half full of water. Cover it and bring to a boil over high heat.

3. Add the salt, oil and fettucine and cook uncovered for about 10 minutes until tender. Stir frequently with the wooden spoon so the noodles won't stick together.
4. Meanwhile, put the butter and cream into the small pot. Place over medium heat just until the butter melts. Take the pot off the heat and stir in 125 mL grated cheese.
5. Drain the cooked fettucine thoroughly in the colander. Pour it onto the warm platter; then pour the sauce over it. Toss lightly with 2 forks to mix.
6. Sprinkle the fettucine with the 50 mL grated cheese and the chopped parsley. Serve at once. Makes 6 servings.

Meat Loaf with Ketchup Sauce

Once it's in the oven, the meat loaf makes itself. That means you can put together a big fresh salad and still have time to relax before you call your family to supper. Because of the oats and wheat germ you use less meat, and that means extra money in your pocket. Refrigerate left-over meat loaf and slice it for sandwiches tomorrow.

Food

1	onion
1 kg	ground beef
1	egg
125 mL	wheat germ
250 mL	rolled oats
5 mL	salt
3 mL	pepper
5 mL	dried basil
100 mL	ketchup
5 mL	mustard
3 mL	nutmeg

Tools

knife
cutting board
large bowl
mixing spoon
measures
1.5 L loaf pan
small bowl

Here's How

1. Set the oven at 180°C.
2. Peel the onion and chop it into small pieces. Place it with the ground beef, egg, wheat germ, rolled oats, salt, pepper and basil in the large bowl. Mix thoroughly.
3. Pack the mixture into the loaf pan. Bake for 45 minutes.
4. Meanwhile, make the sauce by combining the ketchup, mustard and nutmeg in the small bowl.
5. Remove the meat loaf from the oven. If fat has collected around the edges, carefully pour it off.
6. Spread the sauce on top and put the meat loaf back into the oven for another 5 minutes. Serves 6 to 8.

Crispy Baked Fish

Wherever people live by the water, they put down nets and lines to catch fish, a flavourful, rich source of protein. If you ever go fishing, be sure to try this recipe with the fish you catch. Any kind of fish fillets can be cooked this way. Try sole, halibut, cod, turbot or Boston bluefish. But be sure to thaw frozen fish first.

Food

- 15 mL butter
- 500 g fish fillets
- 1 egg
- 100 mL fine bread crumbs
- 3 mL salt
- 2 mL paprika
- 1 mL pepper
- 50 mL butter

Tools

- baking sheet
- measures
- 2 small bowls
- fork
- small pot

Here's How

1. Set the oven at 240°C.
2. Use the 15 mL butter to grease the baking sheet.
3. In one bowl beat the egg well with the fork.
4. In the other bowl mix the bread crumbs, salt, paprika and pepper.
5. Use the fork to dip each fish fillet into the egg and then into the bread crumbs. Coat both sides. Lay each fillet on the baking sheet.
6. Melt the 50 mL butter in the small pot; then dribble it lightly over the fish.
7. Bake the fish for 10 minutes. Serve it with lemon wedges to 4 people.

Lemon Chicken

The light tang of fresh lemon is perfect with meat or poultry. It's a secret Greek cooks have known for centuries. You can use breasts, thighs, drumsticks or wings for this lemon-laced recipe. Try it on a warm summer evening with Greek Tomato Salad (p. 23) and crusty bread.

Food

- 1 kg chicken pieces
- 2 lemons
- 15 mL oregano
- 2 mL salt
- 1 mL pepper
- 50 mL butter

Tools

- large bowl
- cutting board
- knife
- juicer
- measures
- mixing spoon
- tongs
- broiling pan
- small pot

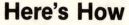

Here's How

1. Place the chicken pieces in the bowl.
2. Cut the lemons in half and squeeze out the juice. Add it to the bowl with the oregano, salt and pepper. Stir well to coat the chicken pieces. Leave this in the refrigerator for 1 hour or longer until you are ready to cook.
3. Arrange the chicken pieces on the broiling pan. Melt the butter in the small pot. Add the liquid from the bowl to the butter and spoon half of this mixture over the chicken pieces.
4. Set the oven to broil. Put the pan about 12 cm below the heating element and broil for 10 minutes. Turn the chicken pieces over, cover with the rest of the butter mixture and broil another 10 minutes. Serves 4.

HINT: This recipe can also be cooked on a barbecue. Place the chicken pieces on the barbecue grill and baste them with the butter mixture as they cook.

Mexico City Ribs

Spice up your life with the hot chili flavour of this Mexican dish. People have grown peppers in Mexico for thousands of years. Mild, sweet or fiery hot, peppers come in many shapes and sizes. The hotter ones, usually called chilies, add zest to many Mexican foods. Chili powder is a mixture of ground, dried chilies and a few milder spices.

Food

- 2 kg spareribs
- 500 mL water
- 250 mL ketchup
- 75 mL Worcestershire sauce
- 10 mL chili powder
- 5 mL salt
- 2 mL Tabasco sauce

Tools

- roasting pan
- measures
- small pot
- large spoon

Here's How

1. Preheat the oven to 220°C.
2. Place the ribs in a shallow roasting pan, meaty side up. Roast for 30 minutes.
3. While the ribs are roasting, measure all the other ingredients into the pot and place over medium heat. Bring this sauce to a boil.
4. Remove the ribs from the oven and pour off any fat that has collected in the pan. Turn the oven temperature down to 160°C.
5. Pour the sauce over the ribs and put them back into the oven for another 45 minutes. Baste frequently. If the sauce dries up, add a little water to the pan during cooking.
6. Cut into serving-size pieces for 5 or 6 people.

Super Burgers

Pity the poor hot dog. He used to be king of the fast foods, but now the hamburger has taken over. Wherever you travel — Paris, Tokyo or Bombay — you'll probably find the hamburger got there first. Once popular just in North America, this sandwich is now being sold around the world. Try these juicy burgers in your own home. Topped with lettuce, tomato and relish, they're a meal all in one.

Food

250 mL cheddar cheese (grated)
1 onion
500 g ground beef
1 egg
50 mL wheat germ
5 mL Worcestershire sauce
2 mL salt
1 mL pepper
6 sesame seed buns
6 pieces of lettuce
1 tomato

Tools

grater
cutting board
knife
measures
large bowl
broiling pan
cookie sheet
lifter

Here's How

1. Grate the cheese. Peel and chop the onion. Combine the cheese and onion with the beef, egg, wheat germ, Worcestershire sauce, salt and pepper in the large bowl. Shape the mixture into 6 patties.
2. Put the patties on the broiling pan. Place the pan about 18 cm from the heat and broil for 5 minutes on each side. Put the buns on the cookie sheet on a lower rack in the oven to warm.

3. Wash and dry the lettuce and tomato. Cut the tomato into 6 slices. Serve each patty on a bun with a piece of lettuce and a tomato slice. Pass the mustard, relish, ketchup, mayonnaise and dill pickles to top it off.

French-Canadian Baked Beans

By the end of the long, cold winter in Quebec the early settlers were probably tired of beans and more beans. But they were grateful for the discovery that dried beans and pork preserved with salt could be stored in large quantities to last from freezeup to spring thaw. Now we have supermarkets and refrigerators to keep us well fed in the winter, but people still enjoy the thick, rich flavour of this traditional dish.

Food

500 g	white pea beans
1 L	water
250 g	salt pork
1	onion
30 mL	brown sugar
25 mL	molasses
5 mL	salt
2 mL	dry mustard
1 mL	pepper

Tools

measures
large pot with lid
colander
bean pot or heavy casserole with lid
cutting board
knife
spoon

Here's How

1. Put the beans and 1 L water into the large pot. Cover it and bring to a boil; then lower the heat and simmer for 20 minutes.

2. Set the oven at 200°C.
3. Drain the beans in the colander. Put them in the bean pot.
4. Cut the salt pork into very small pieces. Stir it in with the beans.
5. Peel the onion and leave it whole. Put it on top of the beans in the pot.
6. Sprinkle the brown sugar, molasses, salt, dry mustard and pepper into the pot without stirring.
7. Add cold water to the pot, just to cover the beans. This will take about 500 mL.
8. Cover the bean pot and bake for 30 minutes. Lower the oven temperature to 120°C and bake for about 4 hours. Check the beans occasionally to see that they stay moist. If they look very dry on top, add 125 mL water. This recipe makes enough for 6 to 8 people.

HINT: If you can't find salt pork in your area, use bacon instead. The flavour will be a bit different, but still very good.

Quick Beef Curry E

Many people believe that curry is a special spice that grows in faraway India. But in fact curry is a mixture of many spices, such as coriander, cumin and turmeric. In India cooks often grind each spice separately and use many different combinations. In Canada we usually buy curry powder that has already been ground and mixed, but it is rarely as zesty as the freshly ground kind.

Food

25 mL vegetable oil
1 large onion
15 mL curry powder
500 g lean ground beef
3 medium tomatoes
5 mL salt
250 mL plain yogurt

Tools

cutting board
knife
frying pan
measures
wooden spoon

Here's How

1. Peel and chop the onion. Place it with the vegetable oil in the frying pan and cook it over medium heat for 5 minutes.
2. Add the curry powder to the frying pan. Cook and stir for 2 minutes.
3. Add the meat; cook and stir until the meat is browned.
4. Wash the tomatoes. Chop them into very small pieces and add to the pan with the salt. Cook, uncovered, for 20 minutes, stirring occasionally.
5. Add the yogurt to the mixture and stir well. Serve at once with Cooked Rice (p. 16) or Chapatis (p. 12) to soak up the sauce. Makes 4 or 5 servings.

HINT: Because curry is spicy, you may want to serve a mild side dish with it. Try banana slices, raisins, unsalted peanuts or coconut as go-togethers.

Portuguese Salt Cod

This recipe has several steps, so you may want to ask someone to share the jobs with you. But the taste is worth the time, as Portuguese families have known for centuries. Remember to start soaking the fish the day before so all the salt will be rinsed out.

Food

500 g	salt cod
4	potatoes
125 mL	olive oil
2	onions
2	garlic cloves
4	hard-cooked eggs (p. 13)
12	black olives
25 mL	chopped parsley

Tools

large pot with lid
colander
measures
cutting board
knife
large frying pan
wooden spoon
large platter

Here's How

1. Put the salt cod into a large pot and cover it with water. Let it soak for 24 hours, but drain it and add fresh water twice on the first day and twice on the day you're going to use it. Now you're ready to cook.
2. Drain the cod in the colander. Wash the potatoes and put them into the pot. Add the cod and cover it all with water. Cover the pot and bring to a boil over high heat. Lower the heat and simmer for 20 minutes until the potatoes and cod are tender.
3. While the cod and potatoes are cooking, peel and slice the onions and garlic. Pour the olive oil into the frying pan and then add the onions and garlic. Cook and stir over medium heat for 10 minutes.
4. Drain the cod and potatoes in the colander. Run cold water over them until they're cool enough to handle.
5. Break the cod into bite-size pieces, removing any skin or bones, and add it to the frying pan. Peel and slice the potatoes and add them to the pan.

6. Gently stir the mixture for 5 to 10 minutes over medium heat to coat it all with oil and to warm it completely.
7. Put the mixture on a warm platter. Peel the hard-cooked eggs; then slice them over the cod and potatoes. Top with black olives and freshly chopped parsley and serve at once. This makes 4 large servings.

East Coast Chowder

Up and down the coast of Atlantic Canada, fish are caught and put in the pot to make this delicious, filling soup. The name "chowder" comes from *chaudière*, which is the French word for a large cooking pot. You can use almost any firm-fleshed fish for this recipe. Cod, halibut, ocean perch and Boston bluefish all make tasty chowders.

Food

- 6 strips bacon
- 2 onions
- 3 potatoes
- 375 mL water
- 5 mL salt
- 1 mL pepper
- 500 g fish fillets
- 500 mL milk
- 25 mL chopped parsley

Tools

- cutting board
- knife
- large pot with lid
- vegetable peeler
- measures

Here's How

1. Peel the onions. Chop the onions and bacon into small pieces. Cook them together in the large pot for 5 minutes over medium heat, stirring often.
2. Peel the potatoes and cut them into thin slices. Add them to the pot with the water, salt and pepper. Cover the pot and bring to a boil; then cook on medium heat for 8 minutes.
3. Cut the fish into bite-size cubes. Add the fish to the pot and cook, covered, another 10 minutes.
4. Add the milk and chopped parsley. Heat the chowder for 5 minutes but don't let it boil. Serve at once. This makes 6 servings.

HINT: If you use frozen fish, you don't have to thaw it. Just cut it into cubes and cook it for 20 minutes instead of 10. (See Step 3.)

 **Sweets and Treats**

Watermelon Granita

Granita is a flavoured ice dessert that is very popular in Italy. But the long, hot days of summer make it just as welcome a treat in Canada. Usually a mixture of water, sugar and flavouring is used, but in this recipe the juicy watermelon provides both the water and the flavouring.

Food

500 mL watermelon
50 mL white sugar
15 mL lemon juice

Tools

spoon
measures
blender
2 L cake pan

Here's How

1. Scoop the watermelon pulp into a glass measure. Be sure to remove all the seeds.
2. Put the watermelon, sugar and lemon juice into the blender jar. Put on the lid and blend at the highest speed until the mixture is liquid.
3. Pour the mixture into the cake pan and freeze it for 3 hours. Scoop small frozen chunks into serving dishes. Makes 6 servings.

Strawberry Ice Cream

Making ice cream is the ideal way to spend a lazy day. But you have to start early if you want ice cream in time for supper. You don't need an ice cream maker. An egg beater or electric mixer and the freezer section of your refrigerator will do the trick. For special snacks cut the ice cream into squares and put it between graham wafers for a cool, sweet sandwich.

Food

- 1 mL small can evaporated milk (160 mL)
- 1 package frozen strawberries (about 425 g)
- 50 mL white sugar
- 15 mL lemon juice

Tools

- measures
- medium bowl
- spoon
- large bowl
- beater
- 2 L cake pan

Here's How

1. Chill the can of milk in the refrigerator and thaw the strawberries in their package at room temperature. This will take about 3 hours.
2. Combine the strawberries and sugar in the medium bowl.
3. Pour the milk and lemon juice into the large bowl and whip with the beater until the mixture stands up in fluffy peaks.
4. Mix the strawberries into the whipped milk. Pour the mixture into the cake pan and freeze it for about 3 hours. This will make 8 large servings.

HINT: For different flavours of ice cream you can substitute either frozen raspberries (thawed) or frozen peaches (thawed and crushed).

Blancmange

This simple pudding is a traditional dessert in Quebec. Eat it plain for everyday meals, or dress it up with rich toppings or special garnishes for the most festive occasions.

Food

750 mL milk
100 mL white sugar
 50 mL cold water
 50 mL cornstarch
  5 mL vanilla

Tools

measures
heavy-bottomed pot
wooden spoon
small mixing bowl
fork
6 small dessert dishes

Here's How

1. Measure the milk and sugar into the pot. Place over medium heat and stir until all the sugar has dissolved.
2. Measure the cold water and cornstarch into the bowl. Stir with the fork until the mixture is perfectly smooth.
3. Turn the heat to low and add the cornstarch mixture to the milk very slowly, stirring constantly until the mixture begins to bubble. This will take about 15 minutes. Remove from the heat and stir in the vanilla.
4. Carefully pour the pudding into the 6 small dishes. Let them sit for 30 minutes before placing them in the refrigerator to chill.

HINT: This pudding may be eaten plain, but it is especially good topped with maple syrup, a fresh strawberry or a dollop of strawberry jam.

Chocolate Cake in a Pan

Chocolate cake is a perfect way to celebrate almost any occasion. So when a family birthday comes along, here's a special treat you can make in a hurry. And there are no messy bowls to clean. What could be easier or more fun to eat?

Food

10 mL butter
375 mL all-purpose flour
250 mL white sugar
50 mL cocoa
5 mL salt
5 mL baking soda
100 mL vegetable oil
15 mL vinegar
5 mL vanilla
250 mL water

Tools

2 L cake pan
measures
wooden spoon

Here's How

1. Set the oven at 190°C.
2. Use the 10 mL butter to grease the cake pan.
3. Measure the flour, sugar, cocoa, salt and baking soda into the cake pan. Stir until well mixed.
4. Make 3 holes in the mixture. Into the first put the vegetable oil, into the second put the vinegar and into the third put the vanilla.
5. Pour the water over the mixture and stir until it is smooth.
6. Put the pan in the oven and bake for 30 minutes.
7. When cool, frost with Peanut Butter Icing (p. 53).

Peanut Butter Icing

Peanut butter was made to go with bread and jelly, bananas, celery and, of course, chocolate cake! This recipe will frost the top of your cake.

Food

100 mL peanut butter
125 mL icing sugar
 25 mL milk
 50 mL peanuts

Tools

small mixing bowl
measures
wooden spoon
knife or spatula

Here's How

1. Measure the peanut butter into the small mixing bowl.
2. Add the icing sugar and stir until it is well mixed.
3. Add the milk, a little at a time, until the icing is smooth and creamy.
4. Use a knife or spatula to spread the icing on your cooled cake.
5. Sprinkle the peanuts on top. You may crush the peanuts first or leave them whole.

Allison's Chocolate Chip Cookies

Before the invention of the chocolate chip in the 1930s, kids knew nothing of the glories of chocolate chip cookies. But we're lucky. We've got chocolate chips *and* Allison's kid-proven recipe.

Food

125 mL butter
100 mL brown sugar
 50 mL white sugar
  1   egg
  5 mL vanilla
250 mL flour (all-purpose or whole wheat)
  2 mL baking soda
  2 mL salt
250 mL chocolate chips (1 small package)

Tools

measures
medium mixing bowl
mixing spoon
small spoon
cookie sheet

Here's How

1. Set the oven at 190°C.
2. Cream together the butter and sugars in the bowl. Stir in the egg and vanilla.
3. Add the flour, baking soda and salt to the bowl. Mix well. Stir in the chocolate chips.
4. Drop the dough by small spoonfuls onto the ungreased cookie sheet, about 5 cm apart. Bake for 8 to 10 minutes until the cookies are lightly browned. Let them cool for 1 minute before removing them from the cookie sheet. This will make about 3 dozen cookies.

HINT: To "cream" ingredients, rub them against the bowl with the back of a spoon until they are soft and fluffy.

Baked Custard with Orange

Custard is probably the most popular dessert in Spain and Portugal. There it is called flan. This version, with the sweet, sharp flavour of fresh orange, is sure to become one of your favourites too.

Food

1 orange
4 eggs
500 mL milk
75 mL white sugar

Tools

grater
large mixing bowl
wire whisk or egg beater
measures
1 L casserole
large baking pan (big enough to hold the casserole)
cutting board
knife

HOW TO INSERT KNIFE IN CENTRE OF BAKED CUSTARD

Here's How

1. Set the oven at 180°C.
2. Wash the orange; then grate the rind into the large bowl. (Be sure to use just the orange part and not the bitter white layer underneath.) Save the rest of the orange for later.
3. Add all of the other ingredients to the bowl and beat lightly. Pour the mixture into the casserole.
4. Set the casserole into the baking pan; then fill the pan almost to the top with warm tap water. Carefully place this in the oven and bake for 55 to 60 minutes. Test the custard by inserting a knife into the centre. If it comes out clean, the custard is done. Remove the casserole from the baking pan to cool the custard.
5. Peel the orange and cut it into thin slices. Arrange the orange slices over the top of the custard. When you serve it, be sure that each helping is topped with orange. This makes 6 servings.

Apple Crisp 🅜

When the days begin to cool and the leaves begin to turn, apples are in season and it's the ideal time for apple crisp. Every fall the boys and girls of Lord Dufferin School in downtown Toronto make this old-fashioned dessert. They use Northern Spies, a great Canadian cooking apple, which softens as it bakes but keeps its plump shape.

Food

- 5 mL shortening
- 4 to 5 large apples (about 1 L when peeled and sliced)
- 50 mL orange juice
- 150 mL brown sugar
- 100 mL all-purpose flour
- 50 mL butter

Tools

- 1 L pie plate
- peeler
- knife
- cutting board
- measures
- small mixing bowl
- pastry blender or 2 knives

Here's How

1. Set the oven at 190°C.
2. Use the shortening to grease the pie plate.
3. Peel the apples, cut them into quarters and remove the cores. Slice them thinly into the pie plate.
4. Pour the orange juice over the apples.
5. Combine the brown sugar and flour in the bowl.
6. Cut in the butter with the pastry blender or 2 knives until the mixture is crumbly. (See illustration, p. 9.) Sprinkle it evenly over the sliced apples.
7. Bake for 35 to 40 minutes until the apples are tender and the top is lightly browned.
8. Let it cool slightly. Makes 6 servings.

Cheesecake Pie

When is a cake a pie? When it's baked and served in a pie plate, of course. This is a quick version of the cheesecake often served as a dessert during the Jewish holidays of Chanukah and Passover.

Food

- 75 mL brown sugar
- 75 mL butter
- 250 mL graham cracker crumbs
- 1 mL nutmeg
- 375 g cream cheese (3 small packages)
- 100 mL white sugar
- 2 eggs
- 2 mL vanilla

Tools

- measures
- small pot
- mixing spoon
- 1 L pie plate
- knife
- mixing bowl
- electric beater
- rubber scraper
- wire rack

Here's How

1. Set the oven at 180°C.
2. Put the brown sugar and butter into the small pot over medium heat. Stir until both are melted. Remove the pot from the heat and add the graham cracker crumbs and the nutmeg. Stir until the crumbs are moistened.
3. Put this mixture into the pie plate. When it is cool enough to touch, use your fingers to press it firmly around the sides and on the bottom. Set aside.
4. Cut each bar of cream cheese into 5 or 6 small pieces. Place the cheese in the bowl; then add the white sugar, eggs and vanilla.
5. Beat at high speed until the mixture is smooth. Scrape it into the crumb-lined pie plate and bake for 25 minutes.
6. Remove from the oven and cool on a wire rack about 1 hour; then put it in the refrigerator until it is thoroughly chilled. Serves 6.

Christmas Carrot Cake

When friends drop by during the holidays, you'll be proud to serve slices of this large, rich cake filled with fruits and nuts. Even though the food list is long, the recipe is simple to put together. And oh so good to eat!

Food

- 5 mL butter
- 10 mL whole wheat flour
- 4 medium carrots (500 mL grated)
- 375 mL brown sugar
- 250 mL vegetable oil
- 4 eggs
- 500 mL mixed dried fruit (1 package)
- 250 mL raisins
- 250 mL walnut pieces
- 750 mL whole wheat flour
- 15 mL baking powder
- 5 mL cinnamon
- 5 mL nutmeg

Tools

- measures
- Bundt pan or 3 L angel food pan
- grater
- large mixing bowl
- mixing spoon
- cutting board
- knife
- medium bowl

Here's How

1. Use the butter to grease the cake pan. Sprinkle it with the 10 mL flour. Tap the pan against the counter to coat it evenly. Shake out any extra flour. Set the oven at 180°C.
2. Grate the carrots. Mix them in the large bowl with the sugar, oil and eggs.
3. Cut up the mixed dried fruit, making sure to remove any prune pits. Add the mixed dried fruit, raisins and walnuts to the carrot mixture.

4. Measure the flour, baking powder, cinnamon and nutmeg into the medium bowl. Stir to blend. Add this to the carrot mixture and stir until well mixed.
5. Pour the batter into the cake pan and bake for 1 hour. Let it cool in the pan. If it is well wrapped, this cake will keep in the refrigerator for a week, or it can be frozen for longer storage.

Fresh Fruit Milkshakes

A tall, cool milkshake is a luscious way to enjoy the unique flavour of fresh strawberries — or any other of your favourite fruits. Try blueberries, peaches or raspberries in the summer, and during the winter months try this recipe again with bananas or any frozen or well-drained canned fruit.

Food
125 mL strawberries
375 mL vanilla ice cream
150 mL milk

Tools
measures
sieve
knife
cutting board
scoop
electric blender

Here's How

1. Put the strawberries into the sieve and rinse them under cold running water. Remove the stems.
2. Slice the berries thinly and place in the blender. Add the ice cream and the milk.
3. Put on the lid and blend for about 30 seconds. Pour at once into 2 tall glasses. This recipe makes a thick shake. For thinner shakes you can use up to 100 mL more milk.

Go-Togethers

Here are a few examples of foods that taste particularly good together. For a well-balanced meal include something from each of the food groups. Foods we have suggested to complete the groups are shown in parentheses. Add your choice of dessert or beverage to round out each meal.

Chinese Dinner

	Page
Chinese Chicken Wings	35
Fried Rice	17
Stir-Fried Broccoli	33
(Milk)	

Indian Dinner

	Page
Quick Beef Curry	45
Cucumber-Yogurt Salad	22
Chapatis or	12
Cooked Rice	16
(Fresh Fruit)	

Portuguese Supper

Portuguese Salt Cod	46
Great Garden Salad	24
(Crusty Rolls)	
Baked Custard with Orange	55

Light Italian Supper

Noodles Alfredo*	36
(Crusty Bread)	
Great Garden Salad	24
Watermelon Granita	49

French-Canadian Supper

French-Canadian Baked Beans**	43
Great Garden Salad	24
Oatmeal Batter Bread	10
Blancmange	51

Greek Lunch

Lemon Chicken	40
Greek Tomato Salad	23
(Crusty Bread)	

Weekend Breakfast

	Page
(Juice)	
Blueberry Pancakes	19
Maple-Flavoured Syrup	19

Picnic Time

Devilled Eggs	15
French Potato Salad	30
Fresh Vegetables	25
Cheese Biscuits	9
Chocolate Chip Cookies	54

Friends For Supper

Meat Loaf with Ketchup Sauce	38
Baked Potatoes with Onion	32
Great Garden Salad	24
Cheesecake Pie	57

Party Time

	Page
Jamaican Patties	20
Fresh Vegetables	25
Three-Cheese Dip	27
Chocolate Cake in Pan with Peanut Butter Icing**	52-53
Fresh Fruit Milkshakes	59

Backyard Barbecue

Super Burgers	42
Corn on the Cob	31
Fresh Fruit Milkshakes	59

Maritime Menu

East Coast Chowder	48
Fresh Vegetables	25
Oatmeal Batter Bread	10
Apple Crisp	56

Remember, there are lots of delicious combinations possible. It's not necessary to stick to the recipes of just one country for a meal. Fried Rice tastes just as good with Lemon Chicken or Jamaican Patties as it does with Chinese Chicken Wings. Great Garden Salad tastes good with anything.

You're on your own now. Cook, eat and enjoy!

---

*Cheese is both a milk product and a meat alternate.

**Dried beans and peanuts are considered meat alternates because of their high protein content.

Measures

Cups and teaspoons are out! Canadians are now using metric measures for cooking. While some ingredients, such as meat, are measured by weight, most are measured by volume using these tools:

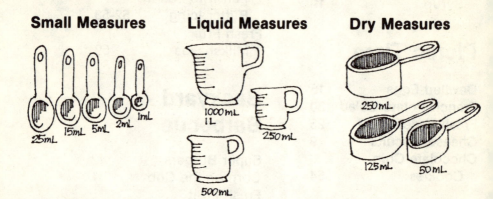

Small Measures: 25 mL, 15 mL, 5 mL, 2 mL, 1 mL

Liquid Measures: 1000 mL (1 L), 250 mL, 500 mL

Dry Measures: 250 mL, 125 mL, 50 mL

Baking Pan Sizes

Baking pans are now measured in litres. To find out the size of a pan or dish you already have, fill it with water from a metric measure and see how much you need to fill it to the top. For example, if your square cake pan holds 2 litres of water to the top, it would be called a 2 L cake pan.

Temperature Conversion

Fahrenheit	Celsius
200° F	100° C
250° F	120° C
300° F	150° C
325° F	160° C
350° F	180° C
375° F	190° C
400° F	200° C
425° F	220° C
450° F	230° C
475° F	240° C

Index

Allison's Chocolate Chip
  Cookies 54
Apple Crisp 56
Bacon Biscuits 9
Baked Custard with
  Orange 55
Baked Potatoes with
  Onion 32
Baking Pan Sizes 62
Biscuits and Breads
  Bacon Biscuits 9
  Campfire Biscuits 9
  Chapatis 12
  Cheese Biscuits 9
  Grandma's Bran Muffins 7
  Oatmeal Batter Bread 10
  Speedy Drop Biscuits 9
  Tea Biscuits 8
  Whole Wheat Biscuits 9
Blancmange 51
Blueberry Pancakes 19
Campfire Biscuits 9
Chapatis 12
Cheese Biscuits 9
Cheesecake Pie 57
Chinese Chicken Wings 35
Chocolate Cake in a Pan 52
Christmas Carrot Cake 58
Coleslaw 29
Cooked Rice 16
Corn on the Cob 31
Crispy Baked Fish 39
Cucumber-Yogurt Salad 22
Desserts
  Apple Crisp 56
  Baked Custard with
    Orange 55
  Blancmange 51
  Cheesecake Pie 57
  Chocolate Cake in a
    Pan 52
  Chocolate Chip Cookies 54

Christmas Carrot Cake 58
Strawberry Ice Cream 50
Watermelon Granita 49
Devilled Eggs 15
East Coast Chowder 48
Egg Salad 14
Favourite Pancakes 18
French-Canadian Baked
  Beans 43
French Potato Salad 30
Fresh Fruit Milkshakes 59
Fresh Vegetables for Dips 25
Fried Rice 17
Go-Togethers 60
Grandma's Bran Muffins 7
Great Garden Salad 24
Greek Tomato Salad 23
Hard-Cooked Eggs 13
Jamaican Patties 20
June's Coleslaw 29
Lemon Chicken 40
Main Dishes
  Chinese Chicken Wings 35
  Crispy Baked Fish 39
  French-Canadian Baked
    Beans 43
  Lemon Chicken 40
  Meat Loaf with Ketchup
    Sauce 38
  Mexico City Ribs 41
  Noodles Alfredo 36
  Portuguese Salt Cod 46
  Quick Beef Curry 45
  Super Burgers 42
Maple-Flavoured Syrup 19
Measures 62
Meat Loaf with Ketchup
  Sauce 38
Mexico City Ribs 41
Noodles Alfredo 36
Oatmeal Batter Bread 10
Pancakes
  Blueberry Pancakes 19
  Favourite Pancakes 18

Peanut Butter Icing 53
Portuguese Salt Cod   46
Quick Beef Curry   45
Red French Dressing   28
Rice
  Cooked Rice   16
  Fried Rice   17
Salads
  Cucumber-Yogurt
    Salad   22
  French Potato Salad   30
  Great Garden Salad   24
  Greek Tomato Salad   23
  June's Coleslaw   29
Speedy Drop Biscuits   9
Stir-Fried Broccoli   33
Strawberry Ice Cream   50
Super Burgers   42
Sweet and Sour Red
  Cabbage   34
Tea Biscuits   8
Temperature Conversion   62
Three-Cheese Dip   27
Vegetables
  Baked Potatoes with
    Onion   32
  Corn on the Cob   31
  Fresh Vegetables for
    Dips   25
  Stir-Fried Broccoli   33
  Sweet and Sour Red
    Cabbage   34
Watermelon Granita   49
Whole Wheat Biscuits   9